Presented to:

_____

From:

_____

Helen Steiner Rice

God Bless America

Compiled by Virginia J. Ruehlmann

Photography by Bill Engel

Fleming H. Revell Company
Tarrytown, New York

ISBN 0-8007-1652-3

Photographs copyright © Bill Engel
Copyright © 1991 by Virginia J. Ruehlmann
and the Helen Steiner Rice Foundation
Published by the Fleming H. Revell Company
Tarrytown, New York 10591
Printed in the United States of America

God knows no strangers, He loves us all
The poor, the rich, the great, the small.
He is a Friend who is always there
To share our troubles and lessen our care.
No one is a stranger in God's sight,
For God is love and in His light
May we, too, try in our small way
To make new friends from day to day.

Whatever the celebration, whatever the day, whatever the event, whatever the occasion, Helen Steiner Rice possessed the ability to express the appropriate feeling for that particular moment in time.

A happening became happier, a sentiment more sentimental, a memory more memorable because of her deep sensitivity to put into understandable language the emotion being experienced. Her positive attitude, her concern for others, and her love of God are identifiable threads woven into her life, her works . . . and even her death.

Prior to her passing, she established the HELEN STEINER RICE FOUNDATION, a nonprofit corporation whose purpose is to award grants to worthy charitable programs that aid the elderly, the needy, and the poor. In her lifetime, these were the individuals about whom Mrs. Rice was greatly concerned.

Royalties from the sale of this book will add to the financial capabilities of the HELEN STEINER RICE FOUNDATION, thus making possible additional grants to various, qualified, worthwhile, and charitable programs. Because of her foresight, her caring, and her deep convictions, Helen Steiner Rice continues to touch a countless number of lives. The continued publication of her poetry in book form by the Fleming H. Revell Company helps to keep Helen's dream alive.

Virginia J. Ruehlmann, Administrator
The Helen Steiner Rice Foundation

Dedicated to the brave and courageous men and women
who served in the past,
are serving in the present,
and will serve in the future
to protect our country
and the principles on which it was founded.
We pray for their safety and well-being,
for their loved ones,
and for peace in our world.

Contents

Introduction

Patriotism takes many forms and is strengthened and expressed in a variety of ways. Love of God and love of our country have been integral concepts with the people of the United States of America since the founding of our nation. Our forefathers believed in those principles and laid the cornerstone for all future generations' freedoms by punctuating the pages of history with the rights of the individual to love God and country. Of such vital importance were these truths that they were declared as being ''self-evident'' by the writers of our Declaration of Independence.

The sight of our country's flag unfurled and flying in the breeze, a stirring rendition of the ''Star-Spangled Banner,'' the Pledge of Allegiance delivered with feeling—all evoke a deepening of our patriotic pride.

Who among us has not had at least one tear come to our eyes, or placed our hand over our heart, or had our emotions swell with pride as we watched a military parade composed of divisions of uniformed representatives—male and female—of all branches of the service, groups of veterans of all ages and wars, and members of various auxiliaries marching in step to the roll of the drums?

God Bless America contains material that we hope will inspire you, will add to your own inventory of prayers, and will assist you to recall some important patriotic moments in the history of our nation. The privileges and rights that we enjoy today were made possible by the sacrifices of our forefathers and men and women whose dedication to God and to our country prevailed through turbulent years.

Now, as never before, let us reaffirm our commitment to maintain the freedoms on which our country was founded and to work for peace in our troubled world.

VIRGINIA J. RUEHLMANN

11

"The
Land of
the
Free"

The Star-Spangled Banner

O say, can you see, by the dawn's early light,
 What so proudly we hailed at the twilight's last gleaming:
Whose broad stripes and bright stars through the perilous fight,
 O'er the ramparts we watched were so gallantly streaming,
And the rockets' red glare, the bombs bursting in air,
Gave proof through the night that our flag was still there;

 O say, does that Star-spangled Banner yet wave
 O'er the land of the free and the home of the brave?

On the shore, dimly seen through the mists of the deep,
 Where the foe's haughty host in dread silence reposes,
What is that which the breeze, o'er the towering steep,
 As it fitfully blows, half conceals, half discloses?
Now it catches the gleam of the morning's first beam—
In full glory reflected, now shines on the stream;

 'Tis the Star-spangled Banner, O long may it wave
 O'er the land of the free and the home of the brave.

And where is that band who so vauntingly swore
 That the havoc of war and the battle's confusion
A home and a country should leave us no more?
 Their blood has washed out their foul footsteps' pollution.
No refuge could save the hireling and slave
From the terror of flight or the gloom of the grave!

 And the Star-spangled Banner in triumph doth wave
 O'er the land of the free and the home of the brave.

O thus be it ever when free men shall stand
 Between their loved homes and the foe's desolation;
Bless'd with victory and peace, may our Heaven-rescued land
 Praise the Power that hath made and preserved us a nation.
Then conquer we must, when our cause it is just—
 And this be our motto—''In God is our trust!''

 And the Star-spangled Banner in triumph shall wave
 O'er the land of the free and the home of the brave.

Francis Scott Key

During the War of 1812 with England, Francis Scott Key, a Maryland lawyer, was authorized by President James Madison to seek the release of a physician friend who had been taken prisoner by the British.

England had already captured Washington and had burned the Capitol and the White House. In September 1814, the British were moving north to demolish Fort McHenry and then occupy Baltimore.

Francis Scott Key received permission to talk with the British admiral on his ship, but he boarded the ship as preparations were being made to attack Fort McHenry. Consequently, the British would not permit him to leave until after the battle.

The battle began in the early hours of September 13 and continued an entire day. Key watched the bombardment of the fort from the British vessel. With the burst of each bomb, rocket, and shell, suspense heightened. During the hours of darkness, he could not tell if the American flag was still flying over the American fort. But "by the dawn's early light," he once again saw that "our flag was still there."

Deeply moved, he scribbled his thoughts on an envelope and later completed the poem that we know today as "The Star-Spangled Banner."

In 1931, more than one hundred years later, "The Star-Spangled Banner" was proclaimed the National Anthem of the United States by the U.S. Congress.

God Bless America

''America the Beautiful''—
May it always stay that way
But to keep Old Glory flying
There's a price that we must pay.
For everything worth having
Demands work and sacrifice,
And freedom is a gift from God
That commands the highest price.
For all our wealth and progress
Are as worthless as can be
Without the faith that made us great
And kept our country free.
Nor can our nation hope to live
Unto itself alone,
For the problems of our neighbors
Must today become our own.
And while it's hard to understand
The complexities of war,
Each one of us must realize
That we are fighting for
The principles of freedom
And the decency of man,
And as a God-loving nation
We're committed to God's plan.
And as the land of liberty
And a great God-fearing nation
We must protect our honor
And fulfill our obligation.
So in these times of crisis
Let us offer no resistance
In giving help to those who need
Our strength and our assistance—
And ''The Stars and Stripes Forever''
Will remain a symbol of
A rich and mighty nation
Built on faith and truth and love.

In God Is Our Strength

It's a troubled world we live in
   and we wish that we might find
Not only happiness of heart
   but longed-for peace of mind.
But where can we begin our search
   in this age of automation
With neighbor against neighbor
   and nation against nation,
Where values have no permanence
   and change is all around
And everything is sinking sand
   and nothing solid ground?
In our fight for freedom
   let us not forget one thing,
The battle is the Lord's
   for He still is the King.
He knows our every purpose,
   and God is on our side
For the things that we fight for
   are right and justified.
Our principles are high
   so we can count upon the Lord
To give us strength and courage
   and His love as a reward.

. . . *"Great and wonderful are thy deeds, O Lord God the Almighty! Just and true are thy ways, O King of the ages!"*

Revelation 15:3

In God We Trust

O God, our help in ages past,
   our hope in years to be,
Look down upon this present
   and see our need of Thee,
For in this age of unrest,
   with danger all around,
We need Thy hand to lead us
   to higher, safer ground,
We need Thy help and counsel
   to make us more aware
That our safety and security
   lie solely in Thy care,
And as we fight for freedom
   make our way and purpose clear
And in our hours of danger
   may we feel Thy presence near.

Seek the Lord and his strength, seek his presence continually!

Psalm 105:4

There Are No Words

Our shock is too great
   our grief is too new
Our emotions too mixed
   our small words too few,
To capture and phrase
   in a fitting expression
All that we've learned
   from this grim tragic lesson.
So while grief is so keen
   and emotion so great,
Let us kneel down in prayer
   as our souls meditate
On the part that we played
   in our nation's decay
That brought us in sorrow
   to this world-shaking day,
Let us search our own souls
   and look deep inside
And see written there
   our vain, selfish pride . . .
For the struggle ahead
   is centered within
Each man has his own
   private battle to win
And above the drum's roll
   and the unrestrained tears
May the words of the Lord
   ring clear in our ears:
"Love one another
   and help those in need,"
Regardless of color
   or race, church, or creed
And keep us both humble
   and grateful, dear God,
Aware of those sleeping
   'neath Arlington's sod

And strengthen the bonds
    that join us with others
So all men may live
    in peace with their brothers
Forgive our transgressions
    and be with us yet
Lest we forget! Lest we forget!

Written after the assassination of President John F. Kennedy.

Let love be genuine; hate what is evil, hold fast to what is good; love one another with brotherly affection; outdo one another in showing honor.
Romans 12:9, 10

A Tribute to John F. Kennedy

His gallant soul has but taken flight
Into the land where there is no night.
He is not dead, he has only gone on
Into a brighter and more wonderful dawn.
For his passion for justice among men of goodwill
No violence can silence, no bullet can still.
For his spirit lives on and, like the warm sun,
It will nourish the dreams that he had begun.
So this hour of sorrow is only God's will,
For the good in this man is living here still. . .
Forgive our transgressions and revive us anew
So we may draw closer to each other and You.
For unless "God is guard," John Kennedy said,
"We're standing unguarded" with dreams that are dead.
For a nation too proud to kneel down and pray
Will crumble to chaos and descend to decay.
So use what He gave for a rededication
And make this once more a God-fearing nation—
A symbol of hope and a standard for good
As we lead in the struggle for a new brotherhood!

*"And I will make of you a great nation, and I will bless you, and make
your name great, so that you will be a blessing."*

Genesis 12:2

God of Creation
Save Our Nation

Great God the Father of all creation,
  Look down upon this strife-torn nation,
Revive our spirits lain dormant so long,
  Renew our faith and keep it strong,
Forgive our arrogance and greed
  And guide us in this hour of need.
Hand of God reach out once more
  And with the "breath of life" restore
Your spirit in the flesh of men
  So we may live in peace again.
For mankind's future and survival
  Depend alone on the spirit's revival!

But as for me, I will look to the Lord, I will wait for the God of my salvation; my God will hear me.

Micah 7:7

Keep America in Your Care

We are faced with many problems
    that grow bigger day by day
And, as we seek to solve them
    in our own self-sufficient way,
We keep drifting into chaos
    and our avarice and greed
Blinds us to the answer
    that would help us in our need . . .
O God, renew our spirit
    and make us more aware
That our future is dependent
    on sacrifice and prayer,
Forgive us our transgressions
    and revive our faith anew
So we may all draw closer
    to each other and to You . . .
For when a nation is too proud
    to daily kneel and pray
It will crumble into chaos
    and descend into decay,
So stir us with compassion
    and raise our standards higher
And take away our lust for power
    and make our one desire
To be a shining symbol
    of all that's great and good
As You lead us in our struggle
    toward newfound brotherhood!

Blessed is the nation whose God is the Lord, the people whom he has chosen as his heritage!

Psalm 33:12

A Prayer for Independence Day

God bless America and keep us safe and free,
Safe from "all our enemies" wherever they may be.
For enemies are forces that often dwell within,
Things that seem so harmless become a major sin,
Little acts of selfishness grow into lust and greed
And make the love of power our idol and our creed . . .
For all our wealth and progress are as
worthless as can be
Without the faith that made us great
and kept our nation free,
And while it's hard to understand the
complexities of war,
Each one of us must realize that we are fighting for
The principles of freedom and the decency of man,
But all of this must be achieved according
to God's plan.
So help us as Americans to search deep down inside
And discover if the things we do are always justified,
And teach us to walk humbly and closer in Thy ways
And give us faith and courage
and put purpose in our days,
And make each one of us aware that each
must do his part
For in the individual is where peace must
have its start.
For a better world to live in where all are
safe and free
Must start with faith and hope
and love deep in the heart of "me."

Righteousness exalts a nation, but sin is a reproach to any people.
Proverbs 14:34

"One Nation Under God"

Thanksgiving is more
   than a day in November
That students of history
   are taught to remember,
More than a date
   that we still celebrate
With turkey and dressing
   piled high on our plate . . .
For while we still offer
   the traditional prayer,
We pray out of habit
   without being aware
That the Pilgrims thanked God
   just for being alive,
For the strength that He gave them
   to endure and survive

Hunger and hardship
   that's unknown in the present
Where progress and plenty
   have made our lives pleasant . . .
And living today
   in this great and rich nation
That depends not on God
   but on mechanization,
We tend to forget
   that our forefathers came
To establish a country
   under God's name . . .
But we feel we're so strong
   we no longer need *faith,*
And it now has become
   nothing more than a wraith
Of the faith that once founded
   this powerful nation
In the name of the Maker
   and the Lord of creation . . .
Oh, teach us, dear God,
   we are all *pilgrims* still,
Subject alone
   to Your guidance and will,
And show us the way
   to purposeful living
So we may have reason
   for daily thanksgiving—
And make us once more
   a *God-fearing nation*
And not just a puppet
   of controlled automation.

The sacrifice of the wicked is an abomination to the Lord, but the prayer of the upright is his delight.

Proverbs 15:8

A Memorial Day Prayer

They served and fought and died
   so that we might be safe and free,
Grant them, O Lord, eternal peace
   and give them the victory!
And in these days of unrest,
   filled with grave uncertainty,
Let's not forget the price they paid
   to keep our country free . . .
And so, on this Memorial Day,
   we offer up a prayer—
May the people of all nations
   be united in Thy care,
And grant us understanding
   and teach us how to live
So we may lose our selfish pride
   and learn to love and give,
And keep us ever mindful
   of the fighting men who sleep
In Arlington and foreign lands
   so we may ever keep
The light of freedom burning
   in their honor through the years
And hear their cry for peace on earth
   resounding in our ears—
Forgive us our transgressions
   and, God, be with us yet
Lest in our pride and arrogance
   we heedlessly forget.

*May we shout for joy over your victory, and in the name of our God set up
our banners! . . .*

Psalm 20:5

28

A Thanksgiving Day Prayer

''Faith of Our Fathers'' renew us again
And make us a nation of God-fearing men
Seeking Thy guidance, Thy love, and Thy will,
For we are but pilgrims in need of Thee still—
And, gathered together on Thanksgiving Day,
May we lift up our hearts and our hands as we pray
To thank You for blessings we so little merit
And grant us Thy love and teach us to share it.

The Lord is my strength and my shield; in him my heart trusts; so I am
helped, and my heart exults, and with my song I give thanks to him.

Psalm 28:7

Battle Hymn of the Republic

Mine eyes have seen the glory of the coming of the Lord;
He is trampling out the vintage where the grapes of wrath are stored;
He hath loosed the fateful lightning of His terrible swift sword—
His truth is marching on.

I have seen Him in the watchfires of a hundred circling camps,
They have builded Him an altar in the evening dews and damps;
I can read His righteous sentence by the dim and flaring lamps—
His day is marching on.

He has sounded forth the trumpet that shall never sound retreat,
He is sifting out the hearts of men before His judgment seat;
O be swift, my soul, to answer Him! be jubilant, my feet!—
Our God is marching on.

In the beauty of the lilies Christ was born across the sea,
With a glory in His bosom that transfigures you and me;
As He died to make men holy, let us die to make men free—
While God is marching on.

Refrain
Glory! glory, hallelujah!
Glory! glory, hallelujah!
Glory! glory, hallelujah!
His truth is marching on.

JULIA WARD HOWE

In 1861, Washington, D.C., was pulsating with tension, anticipating the Civil War. This was the year that Julia Ward Howe and her husband, Samuel Gridley Howe, arrived there.

They witnessed soldiers marching off to battle. One day they were invited by President Lincoln to witness a review of the Union soldiers, but before the review began, Southern troops broke up the ceremony. The war preparations alarmed Mrs. Howe, and she was also troubled by the popular song, "John Brown's Body Lies a Mould'ring in the Grave," which she heard sung by soldiers as they marched by her hotel.

Knowing her concern, a minister friend suggested, "If you are so concerned about the singing of that song, why don't you write some decent words for the tune?"

"I will," she replied. The words came to her that night.

"I awoke in the gray of the morning, and as I lay waiting for dawn, the long lines of the desired poem began to entwine themselves in my mind." So she got up quickly, found "an old stump of a pen," and wrote the words of the "Battle Hymn of the Republic."

She submitted the poem to the *Atlantic Monthly* magazine and was paid five dollars for it. It was published early in 1862.

Later this hymn was sung by a Civil War chaplain at a rally attended by President Abraham Lincoln. When the singer had finished and the applause had diminished, President Lincoln sent a note to the platform with the request, "Sing it again." The chaplain sang it again with the audience joining in the refrain.

Soon the entire nation was singing the song.

Important Words

We all need words to live by,
To inspire us and guide us,
Words to give us courage
When the trials of life betide us—
And the words that never fail us
Are the words of God above,
Words of comfort and of courage
Filled with wisdom and with love—
They are ageless and enduring,
They have lived through generations,
There's no question left unanswered
In our Father's revelations—
And in this ever-changing world
God's words remain unchanged,
For though through countless ages
They've been often rearranged
The truth shines through all changes
Just as bright today as when
Our Father made the universe
And breathed His life in men—
So whenever you are troubled
And your heart is sad with sorrow,
You'll find comfort, strength, and courage
To help you meet tomorrow
If you will cast your burden
Completely on the Lord,
For faith that does not falter
Will bring its own reward—
And through the darkest hours
Of deep discouragement,
God is your strength and refuge
And your soul's encouragement.

Seek His Guidance

Refuse to be discouraged,
Refuse to be distressed,
For when we are despondent
Our life cannot be blessed,
For doubt and fear and worry
Close the door to faith and prayer,
For there's no room for blessings
When we're lost in deep despair,
So remember when you're troubled
With uncertainty and doubt
It is best to tell our Father
What our fear is all about,
For unless we seek His guidance
When troubled times arise
We are bound to make decisions
That are twisted and unwise.

"For I know the plans I have for you, says the Lord, plans for welfare and not for evil, to give you a future and a hope. Then you will call upon me and come and pray to me, and I will hear you."

Jeremiah 29:11, 12

Great Faith That Smiles
Is Born of Great Trials

It's easy to say, "In God we trust,"
When life is radiant and fair,
But the test of faith is only found
When there are burdens to bear.
For our claim to faith in the sunshine
Is really no faith at all,
For when roads are smooth and days are bright
Our need for God is small,
And no one discovers the fullness
Or the greatness of God's love
Unless they have walked in the darkness
With only a light from above.
For the faith to endure whatever comes
Is born of sorrow and trials,
And strengthened only by discipline
And nurtured by self-denials.
So be not disheartened by troubles,
For trials are the building blocks
On which to erect a fortress of faith
Secure on God's ageless rocks.

Yea, thou art my rock and my fortress; for thy name's sake lead me and guide me, take me out of the net which is hidden for me, for thou art my refuge.

Psalm 31:3, 4

Faith Is a Mighty Fortress

We look ahead through each changing year
With mixed emotions of
Hope and fear,
Hope for the peace we long have sought,
Fear that our hopes
   will come to naught . . .
Unwilling to trust in the Father's will
We count on our logic and shallow skill
And, in our arrogance and pride,
Man is no longer satisfied
To place his confidence and love
With childlike faith
   in God above . . .
But tiny hands and tousled heads
That kneel in prayer by little beds
Are closer to the dear Lord's heart
And of His kingdom
   more a part
Than we who search and never find
The answers to our questioning mind,
For faith in things we cannot see
Requires a child's simplicity . . .
O Father, grant once more to men
A simple childlike faith again.

For this very reason make every effort to supplement your faith with virtue, and virtue with knowledge, and knowledge with self-control, and self-control with steadfastness, and steadfastness with godliness, and godliness with brotherly affection, and brotherly affection with love.

2 Peter 1:5–7

God Is Standing By

There are times when life overwhelms us
And our trials seem too many to bear,
It is then we should stop to remember
God is standing by ready to share
The uncertain hours that confront us
And fill us with fear and despair
For God in His goodness has promised
That the cross He gives us to wear
Will never exceed our endurance
Or be more than our strength can bear,
And secure in that blessed assurance
We can smile as we face tomorrow
For God holds the key to the future
And no sorrow or care need we borrow!

People's Problems

Everyone has problems
  in this restless world of care,
Everyone grows weary
  with the cross they have to bear,
Everyone is troubled
  and their skies are overcast
As they try to face the future
  while still dwelling in the past.
But the people with their problems
  only listen with one ear
For people only listen
  to the things they want to hear
And they only hear the kind of things
  they are able to believe
And the answers that are God's to give
  they're not ready to receive,
So while the people's problems
  keep growing every day
And men vainly try to solve them
  in their own self-willful way,
God seeks to help and watches,
  waiting always patiently
To help them solve their problems
  whatever they may be.
So may the people of all nations
  at last become aware
That God will solve the people's problems
  through faith and hope and prayer!

"Call to me and I will answer you, and will tell you great and hidden things which you have not known."

Jeremiah 33:3

Basic Training

Father, I have knowledge,
  so will You show me now
How to use it wisely
  and find a way somehow
To make the world I live in
  a little better place,
And make life with its problems
  a bit easier to face.
Grant me faith and courage
  and put purpose in my days,
And show me how to serve Thee
  in the most effective ways
So that all my training,
  my knowledge, and my skill,
May find their true fulfillment
  as I learn to do Thy will.
And may I ever be aware
  in everything I do
That knowledge comes from learning
  and wisdom comes from You.

Happy is the man who finds wisdom, and the man who gets understanding, for the gain from it is better than gain from silver and its profit better than gold.

Proverbs 3:13, 14

Everybody Everywhere Needs
Somebody Sometime

Everybody, everywhere,
  no matter what his station,
Has moments of deep loneliness
  and quiet desperation,
For this lost and lonely feeling
  is inherent in mankind—
It is just the Spirit speaking
  as God tries again to find
An opening in the worldly wall
  man builds against God's touch,
For he feels so self-sufficient
  that he does not need God much,
So he vainly goes on struggling
  to find some explanation
For these disturbing, lonely moods
  of inner isolation . . .
But the answer keeps eluding him
  for in his selfish, finite mind
He does not even recognize
  that he cannot ever find
The reason for life's emptiness
  unless he learns to share
The problems and the burdens
  that surround him everywhere—
But when his eyes are opened
  and he looks with love at others
He begins to see not strangers
  but understanding brothers . . .
So open up your hardened hearts
  and let God enter in—
He only wants to help you
  a new life to begin . . .
And every day's a good day
  to lose yourself in others

And anytime a good time
   to see mankind as brothers,
And this can only happen
   when you realize it's true
That everyone needs someone
   and that someone is you!

"Give, and it will be given to you; good measure, pressed down, shaken together, running over, will be put into your lap. For the measure you give will be the measure you get back."

Luke 6: 38

43

The Way to God

If my days were untroubled and my heart always light
Would I seek that fair land where there is no night?
If I never grew weary with the weight of my load
Would I search for God's peace at the end of the road?
If I never knew sickness and never felt pain
Would I reach for a hand to help and sustain?
If I walked not with sorrow and lived without loss
Would my soul seek sweet solace at the foot of the cross?
If all I desired was mine day by day
Would I kneel before God and earnestly pray?
If God sent no winter to freeze me with fear
Would I yearn for the warmth of spring every year?
I ask myself this and the answer is plain—
If my life were all pleasure and I never knew pain
I'd seek God less often and need Him much less,
For God's sought more often in times of distress,
And no one knows God or sees Him as plain
As those who have met Him on the pathway of pain.

Many are the afflictions of the righteous; but the Lord delivers him out of them all.

Psalm 34:19

God Knows Best

God never hurts us needlessly,
And He never wastes our pain,
For every loss He sends to us
Is followed by rich gain.
And when we count the blessings
That God has so freely sent,
We will find no cause for murmuring
And no time to lament.
For our Father loves His children,
And to Him all things are plain,
So He never sends us pleasure
When the soul's deep need is pain.
So whenever we are troubled,
And when everything goes wrong,
It is just God working in us
To make our spirit strong.
And every individual,
As well as every nation,
Will find that in adversity
There is always compensation . . .
And men as well as nations
Must take lessons in the school
That teaches by experience
That the plain old Golden Rule
Is still the best to live by,
For its sheer simplicity
Insures a peaceful universe—
And that's our fervent plea.

"And if you obey the voice of the Lord your God, being careful to do all his commandments which I command you this day, the Lord your God will set you high above all the nations of the earth."

Deuteronomy 28:1

Thank You, God,
For Everything

Thank You, God, for everything,
the big things and the small,
For every good gift comes from God,
the Giver of them all,
And all too often we accept
without any thanks or praise
The gifts God sends as blessings
each day in many ways.
First, thank You for the little things
that often come our way,
The things we take for granted
but don't mention when we pray,
Then, thank You for the miracles
we are much too blind to see,
And give us new awareness
of our many gifts from Thee,
And help us to remember
that the key to life and living
Is to make each prayer a prayer of thanks
and every day Thanksgiving.

Let us come into his presence with thanksgiving; let us make a joyful noise to him with songs of praise!

Psalm 95:2

God's Changeless Laws

Man with all his greatness,
  his knowledge, and his skill,
Is still as helpless as a child
  and subject to God's will,
And there is nothing man can do
  to bring lasting joy and peace
Or curb his untamed passions
  or make his longings cease,
But the humble, full acknowledgment
  that there is no substitute
To bring forth a happy harvest
  except the Spirit's fruit,
For unless man's spirit is redeemed
  he will never, ever find
Unblemished love and happiness
  and eternal peace of mind.

Blessings in Disguise

When troubles come
   and things go wrong,
And days are cheerless
   and nights are long,
We find it so easy
   to give in to despair
By magnifying
   the burdens we bear . . .
And the blessing God sent
   in a "darkened disguise"
Our troubled hearts
   fail to recognize
Not knowing God sent it
   not to distress us
But to strengthen our faith
   and redeem us and bless us.

Blessed is the man who endures trial, for when he has stood the test he will receive the crown of life which God has promised to those who love him.
James 1:12

Dark Shadows Fall in the Lives of Us All

Sickness, injury, and sorrow
   come to us all,
But through them we grow
   and learn to stand tall,
For trouble is part
   and parcel of life
And no man can grow
   without struggle and strife,
And the more we endure
   with patience and grace
The stronger we grow
   and the more we can face,
And the more we can face,
   the greater our love,
And with love in our hearts
   we are more conscious of
The pain and the sorrow
   in lives everywhere,
So it is through trouble
   that we learn how to share.

Be merciful to me, O God, be merciful to me, for in thee my soul takes refuge; in the shadow of thy wings I will take refuge, till the storms of destruction pass by.

Psalm 57:1

"Life Liberty, and the Pursuit of Happiness"

In Congress, July 4, 1776
The Unanimous Declaration of the Thirteen United States of America.

When in the Course of human events, it becomes necessary for one people to dissolve the political bands which have connected them with another, and to assume among the powers of the earth, the separate and equal station to which the Laws of Nature and of Nature's God entitle them, a decent respect to the opinions of mankind requires that they should declare the causes which impel them to the separation.

We hold these truths to be self-evident, that all men are created equal, that they are endowed by their Creator with certain unalienable Rights, that among these are Life, Liberty and the Pursuit of Happiness. That to secure these rights, Governments are instituted among Men, deriving their just powers from the consent of the governed. That whenever any Form of Government becomes destructive of these ends, it is the Right of the People to alter or to abolish it, and to institute new Government, laying its foundation on such principles and organizing its powers in such form, as to them shall seem most likely to effect their Safety and Happiness. . . .

DECLARATION OF INDEPENDENCE, 1776

The Preamble to the Constitution

We the people of the United States, in order to form a more perfect Union, establish justice, insure domestic tranquility, provide for the common defense, promote the general welfare, and secure the blessings of liberty to ourselves and our posterity do ordain and establish this Constitution for the United States of America.

CONSTITUTION OF THE UNITED STATES, 1788

Washington's Prayer for Our Country

I now make it my earnest prayer, that God would have you, and the state over which you preside, in His Holy protection; that He would incline the hearts of the citizens to cultivate a spirit of subordination and obedience to Government; to entertain a brotherly affection, and love for one another, for their fellow citizens of the United States at large, and particularly for their brethren who have served in the field, and finally that He would dispose us all to do justice, to love mercy, and to demean ourselves with the characteristics of the Divine Author of our blessed religion, and without a humble imitation of whose example in these things, we can never hope to be a happy nation.

GEORGE WASHINGTON, 1792

Photo: Courtesy of The Freedoms Foundation at Valley Forge.

Words From Our Founding Fathers

"Liberty, when it begins to take root, is a plant of rapid growth."

George Washington

"God grant that not only the love of liberty, but a thorough knowledge of the rights of men may pervade all nations of the earth."

Benjamin Franklin

"I only regret that I have but one life to lose for my country."

Nathan Hale

"The cement of this union is the heart blood of every American."

Thomas Jefferson

"Those who expect to reap the blessings of freedom must, like men, undergo the fatigue of supporting it."

Thomas Paine

"Those who will not be governed by God will be ruled by tyrants."

William Penn

"I know not what course others may take, but as for me, give me liberty, or give me death!"

Patrick Henry

Our Country's Flag

By action of the newly formed Congress, which convened on June 14, 1777, it was resolved: "That the flag of the United States be made of thirteen stripes, alternate red and white; that the Union be thirteen stars, white in a blue field, representing a new constellation."

Through the years, in 1794 and again in 1818, alterations to the flag were required because more states were being admitted to the United States of America. On April 4, 1818, Section Two was added to the Flag Act to establish the permanent flag of the United States.

> Section 2. And be it further enacted that on the admission of every new state into the Union, one star be added to the union of the flag; and that such addition shall take effect on the fourth of July next succeeding such admission.

Little did our forefathers realize that eventually there would be fifty stars in the blue field, creating a magnificent new constellation!

"We take the stars from Heaven, and the red from our mother country, separating it by white stripes, thus showing we have separated from her, and the white stripes go down to posterity representing Liberty."

George Washington

"This flag which we honor and under which we serve is the emblem of our unity, our power, our thought and purpose as a nation. It has no other character than that which we give it from generation to generation. The choice is ours. It floats in majestic silence above the hosts that execute those choices whether in peace or in war. And yet, though silent, it speaks to us—speaks to us of the past, of the men and women who went before us and of the records they wrote upon it. We celebrate the day of its birth; and from its birth until now it has witnessed a great history, has floated on high the symbol of great events, of a great plan of life worked out by a great people."

Woodrow Wilson

"Shoot, if you must, this old gray head, but spare your country's flag."

Barbara Fritchie

Barbara Fritchie, born December 3, 1766, was ninety-six years of age when she proudly displayed her Union flag by hanging it from her upstairs window as Confederate soldiers marched through the streets of Fredericksburg, Maryland, in 1862. She reportedly spoke the above words when orders were given by the commanding officer to shoot down her beloved flag. She and her flag were spared as the officer commanded his troops to "march on." She died December 18, 1862, and was immortalized in the poem "Barbara Frietchie" by John Greenleaf Whittier.

The Pledge of Allegiance

''I pledge allegiance to the flag of the United States of America and to the republic for which it stands, one nation under God, indivisible, with liberty and justice for all.''

Our Pledge of Allegiance was written by a former minister, Francis Bellamy, in 1892, when he was a member of the staff of the *Youth's Companion,* a children's magazine.

Only two noticeable changes have taken place in the wording of the Pledge since its first appearance in the *Youth's Companion.* In 1923, the First National Flag Conference recommended that *my flag* be substituted with the words *the flag of the United States of America,* and on June 14, 1954, President Dwight D. Eisenhower approved a change made by House Joint Resolution 243 which amended the Pledge by adding the words *under God,* so that the Pledge now states, ''one nation under God, indivisible, with liberty and justice for all.''

Photo: Theresa Marshall

The Liberty Bell

The Liberty Bell was first hung in Independence Hall, Philadelphia, in 1753. It bore the inscription, "Proclaim Liberty throughout all the Land unto all the inhabitants Thereof" (Leviticus 25:10), thus, it was fitting that the bell was rung in July 1776 to proclaim the Declaration of Independence. Taken to Allentown and hidden during the British occupation of Philadelphia (1777–78), it was later brought back. In 1781 it was moved from the steeple to the brick tower. It was cracked in 1835 and again in 1846, and rests on its original timbers as an exhibit.

The Gettysburg Address

Fourscore and seven years ago our fathers brought forth on this continent a new nation, conceived in liberty and dedicated to the proposition that all men are created equal.

Now we are engaged in a great civil war, testing whether that nation or any nation so conceived and so dedicated, can long endure. We are met on a great battlefield of that war. We have come to dedicate a portion of that field, as a final resting place for those who here gave their lives that that nation might live. It is altogether fitting and proper that we should do this.

But, in a larger sense, we can not dedicate—we can not consecrate—we can not hallow—this ground. The brave men, living and dead, who struggled here, have consecrated it, far above our poor power to add or detract. The world will little note, nor long remember, what we say here, but it can never forget what they did here. It is for us the living, rather, to be dedicated here to the unfinished work which they who fought here thus far so nobly advanced. It is rather for us to be here dedicated to the great task remaining before us—that from these honored dead we take increased devotion to that cause for which they gave the last full measure of devotion—that we here highly resolve that these dead shall not have died in vain—that this nation, under God, shall have a new birth of freedom— and that government of the people, by the people, for the people, shall not perish from the earth.

ABRAHAM LINCOLN, 1863

The Statue of Liberty

The Statue of Liberty, created by a young French sculptor named Frédéric-Auguste Bartholdi, was a gift from the people of France to the people of America in recognition of the friendship between the two countries. It was dedicated on October 28, 1886.

Liberty Enlightening the World was erected on Bedloe's Island in New York Harbor, a welcoming sight to all who come to America. In her raised right hand, she holds a lamp; in her left, a tablet with the inscription "July 4, 1776." In 1883, Emma Lazarus wrote "The New Colossus" for the pedestal of the statue. It concludes:

> Give me your tired, your poor, your huddled masses yearning to breathe free, the wretched refuse of your teeming shore. Send these, the homeless, tempest-tost to me, I lift my lamp beside the golden door!

In 1956, Bedloe's Island was renamed Liberty Island in accordance with Bartholdi's request prior to his death in 1904.

The Tomb of the Unknown Soldier

There are four soldiers buried in the Tomb of the Unknown Soldier in Arlington Cemetery:

> one representative from World War I
> one representative from World War II
> one representative from the Korean War
> one representative from the Vietnam War

The tomb came into existence in 1921 when the body of an unidentified deceased soldier was selected to represent all of those who had died in World War I. At 11:00 A.M. on November 11, the body was lowered into the tomb. On the tomb are the following words:

> *Here rests in honored glory*
> *An American Soldier*
> *Known only to God.*

The Presidents Speak

"Equal and exact justice to all men . . . freedom of religion; freedom of the press; freedom of person under the protection of the habeas corpus; and trial by juries impartially selected—these principles form the bright constellation which has gone before us."

Thomas Jefferson

———————

"The first requisite of a good citizen in this Republic of ours is that he shall be able and willing to pull his weight."

Theodore Roosevelt

———————

"But the right is more precious than peace, and we shall fight for the things which we have always carried nearest our hearts—for democracy, for the right of those who submit to authority to have a voice in their own governments, for the rights and liberties of small nations, for a universal dominion of right by such a concert of free peoples as shall bring peace and safety to all nations and make the world itself at last free."

Woodrow Wilson

———————

"My country owes me no debt. It gave me, as it gives every boy and girl, a chance. It gave me schooling, independence of action, opportunity for service and honor. In no other land could a boy from a country village without inheritance or influential friends look forward with unbound hope. My whole life has taught me what America means. I am indebted to my country beyond any power to repay."

Herbert Hoover

"We, too, born to freedom and believing in freedom, are willing to fight to maintain freedom. We, and all others who believe as deeply as we do, would rather die on our feet than live on our knees."

Franklin Delano Roosevelt

———————

"We must build a new world, a far better world—one in which the eternal dignity of man is respected."

Harry S. Truman

———————

"Almighty God . . . Give us, we pray, the power to discern clearly right from wrong and allow all our words and actions to be governed thereby, and by the laws of this land. Especially we pray that our concern shall be for all the people regardless of station, race or calling.

"May cooperation . . . be the mutual aim of those who, under the concepts of our Constitution, hold to differing political faiths; so that all may work for the good of our beloved country and Thy glory. Amen."

Dwight D. Eisenhower

———————

"Ask not what your country can do for you—ask what you can do for your country."

John F. Kennedy
(quoting Oliver Wendell Holmes, Jr.)

"Let us learn together and laugh together and work together and pray together, confident that in the end we will triumph together in the right."

Jimmy Carter

"I believe we, the Americans of today, are ready to do what must be done to ensure happiness and liberty for ourselves, our children, and our children's children. And as we renew ourselves here in our land, we will be seen as having greater strength throughout the world. We will again be the exemplar of freedom and a beacon of hope for those who do not now have freedom."

Ronald Reagan

"As Americans, we know there are times when we must step forward and accept our responsibility to lead the world away from the dark chaos of dictators, toward the brighter promise of a better day."

George Bush

The motto of the United States of America

In God We Trust

Officially accepted as our nation's motto on July 30, 1956.

"Crown
Thy Good
With
Brotherhood"

America, the Beautiful

O beautiful for spacious skies,
For amber waves of grain,
For purple mountain majesties
Above the fruited plain!
America! America!
God shed His grace on thee,
And crown thy good with brotherhood
From sea to shining sea.

O beautiful for pilgrim feet,
Whose stern, impassioned stress
A thoroughfare for freedom beat
Across the wilderness!
America! America!
God mend thine ev'ry flaw,
Confirm thy soul in self-control,
Thy liberty in law.

O beautiful for heroes proved
In liberating strife,
Who more than self their country loved
And mercy more than life!
America! America!
May God thy gold refine,
Till all success be nobleness,
And ev'ry gain divine.

O beautiful for patriot dream
That sees, beyond the years,
Thine alabaster cities gleam—
Undimmed by human tears!
America! America!
God shed His grace on thee,
And crown thy good with brotherhood
From sea to shining sea.

KATHERINE LEE BATES

It was in commemoration of the 400th anniversary of the discovery of America that Katherine Lee Bates wrote this patriotic hymn.

Miss Bates and other professors from Wellesley College in Massachusetts traveled to the Midwest and then to the Rocky Mountains in 1893. En route, they stopped in Chicago to see the Columbian Exposition. The stunning alabaster buildings and the brilliantly designed architecture of the Chicago World's Fair impressed them deeply. Leaving Chicago, they were amazed at the "fruited plains" of the midwestern states, but arriving in Colorado Springs, they were overwhelmed by the majesty of Pike's Peak and the entire Rocky Mountain range.

One evening, one of the teachers spoke of her dream of America in the 1900s, where the cities would be of alabaster and all mankind might live together in brotherhood. Katherine Lee Bates looked in both directions, seeing the Great Plains stretch in one direction and the Rockies stretch the other way. "It was there, as I was looking out over the sea-like expanse of fertile country, spreading away so far under the ample skies, that the opening lines of this text formed themselves in my mind."

As she thought about the challenges of the future, she commented, "We must match the greatness of our country with the goodness of personal, godly living." Later that night, Katherine Lee Bates wrote the stanzas of "America, the Beautiful."

The Way to Love and Peace

There is no thinking person
Who can stand untouched today
And view the world around us
Slowly drifting to decay
Without feeling deep within him
A silent, unnamed dread
As he contemplates the future
That lies frighteningly ahead
As the clouds of chaos
Gather in man's muddled mind,
And he searches for the answer
He alone can never find,
Let us recognize we're facing
Problems man has never solved,
And with all our daily efforts
Life grows more and more involved,
But our future will seem brighter
And we'll meet with less resistance
If we call upon our Father
And seek divine assistance
For the spirit can unravel
Many tangled, knotted threads
That defy the skill and power
Of the world's best hands and heads,
And our plans for growth and progress,
Of which we all have dreamed,
Cannot survive materially
Unless our spirits are redeemed
For only when the mind of man
Is united with the soul
Can love and peace combine to make
Our lives complete and whole.

I Think of You and
I Pray for You, Too

Often during a busy day
I pause for a minute
   to silently pray,
I mention the names
   of those I love
And treasured friends
   I am fondest of—
For it doesn't matter
   where we pray
If we honestly mean
   the words that we say,
For God is always
   listening to hear
The prayers that are
   made by a heart that's sincere.

But I, O Lord, cry to thee; in the morning my prayer comes before thee.
Psalm 88:13

"I Am the Light of the World"

In this sick world of hatred
And violence and sin
Where men renounce morals
And reject discipline,
We stumble in darkness,
Groping vainly for light
To distinguish the difference
Between wrong and right,
But dawn cannot follow
This night of despair
Unless faith lights a candle
In all hearts everywhere
And warmed by the glow
Our hate melts away
And love lights the path
To a peaceful, new day.

In Times Like These

We read the headlines daily
  and listen to the news,
We shake our heads despairingly
  and glumly sing the blues,
We are restless and dissatisfied
  and we do not feel secure,
We are vaguely discontented
  with the things we must endure . . .
This violent age we live in
  is filled with nameless fears
As we listen to the newscasts
  that come daily to our ears,
And we view the threatening future
  with sad sobriety
As we're surrounded daily
  by increased anxiety.

How can we find security
   or stand on solid ground
When there's violence and dissension
   and confusion all around?
Where can we go for refuge
   from the rising tides of hate,
Where can we find a haven
   to escape this shameful fate?
So instead of reading headlines
   that disturb the heart and mind,
Let us open up the Bible
   and in doing so we'll find
That this age is no different
   from the millions gone before,
But in every hour of crisis
   God has opened up a door
For all who seek His guidance
   and trust His all-wise plan,
For God provides protection
   beyond that devised by man.
And we learn that each tomorrow
   is not ours to understand,
But lies safely in the keeping
   of the great Creator's hand,
And to have the steadfast knowledge
   that we never walk alone
And to rest in the assurance
   that our every need is known
Will help dispel our worries,
   our anxieties and care,
For doubt and fear are vanquished
   in the peacefulness of prayer.

Offer right sacrifices, and put your trust in the Lord.
Psalm 4:5

Anywhere Is a Place of Prayer If God Is There

I have prayed on my knees in the morning,
I have prayed as I walked along,
I have prayed in the silence and darkness
And I've prayed to the tune of a song.
I have prayed in the midst of triumph
And I've prayed when I suffered defeat,
I have prayed on the sands of the desert
And where the waves of the ocean beat.
I have prayed in a velvet-hushed forest
Where the quietness calmed my fears,
I have prayed through suffering and heartache
When my eyes were blinded with tears.
I have prayed in churches and chapels,
Cathedrals and synagogues, too,
But often I've had the feeling
That my prayers were not getting through.
And I realized then that Our Father
Is not really concerned where we pray
Or impressed by our manner of worship
Or the eloquent words that we say . . .
He is only concerned with our feelings,
And He looks deep into our heart
And hears the cry of our soul's deep need
That no words could ever impart . . .
So it isn't the prayer that's expressive
Or offered in some special spot,
It's the sincere plea of a sinner
And God can tell whether or not
We honestly seek His forgiveness
And earnestly mean what we say,
And then and then only He answers
The prayer that we fervently pray.

In my distress I called upon the Lord; to my God I cried for help. From his temple he heard my voice, and my cry to him reached his ears.

Psalm 18:6

Into God's Hands

There is so little any of us can do,
But I know that God will take care of you.
For He's so great and we're so small,
But He is mindful of us all
And I will say a little prayer
And place you safely in His care.

A Mother's Prayer for Her Loved One
In the Service of Our Country

I said a little prayer for you
   and I asked the Lord above
To keep you safely in His care
   and enfold you in His love.
I did not ask for fortune
   for riches or for fame,
I only asked for blessings
   in the Savior's Holy Name.
Blessings to surround you
   in times of trial and stress
And inner joy to fill your heart
   with peace and happiness.

"And whatever you ask in prayer, you will receive, if you have faith."
Matthew 21:22

A Prayer for Peace

Our Father, up in heaven,
    hear this fervent prayer:
May the people of *all nations*
    be *united* in *Thy care,*
For earth's peace and man's salvation
    can come only by thy grace
And not through bombs and missiles
    and our quest for outer space . . .
For until all men recognize
    that *"the battle is the Lord's"*
And peace on earth cannot be won
    with strategy and swords,
We will go on vainly fighting,
    as we have in ages past,
Finding only empty victories
    and a peace that cannot last . . .
But we've grown so rich and mighty
    and so arrogantly strong,
We no longer ask in humbleness—
    "God, show us where we're wrong" . . .
We have come to trust completely
    in the power of man-made things,
Unmindful of God's mighty power
    and that *He* is *"King of Kings"* . . .
We have turned our eyes away from *Him*
    to go our selfish way,
And money, power, and pleasure
    are the gods we serve today . . .
And the good green earth God gave us
    to peacefully enjoy,
Through greed and fear and hatred
    we are seeking to **destroy** . . .

O Father, up in heaven,
   stir and wake our sleeping souls,
Renew our faith and lift us up
   and give us higher goals,
And grant us heavenly guidance
   as war threatens us again
For, more than *guided missiles,*
All the world needs *guided men.*

He makes wars cease to the end of the earth; he breaks the bow, and shatters the spear, he burns the chariots with fire!

Psalm 46:9

Never Be Discouraged

There is really nothing we need know
　　or even try to understand
If we refuse to be discouraged
　　and trust God's guiding hand.
So take heart and meet each minute
　　with faith in God's great love,
Aware that every day of life
　　is controlled by God above.
So never dread tomorrow
　　or what the future brings,
Just pray for strength and courage
　　and trust God in all things.
And never grow discouraged
　　be patient and just wait
For God never comes too early
　　and He never comes too late!

The works of his hands are faithful and just; all his precepts are trustworthy, they are established for ever and ever, to be performed with faithfulness and uprightness.

Psalm 111:7, 8

God, Are You There?

I'm way down here!
  You're way up there!
Are You sure You can hear
  My faint, faltering prayer?
For I'm so unsure
  Of just how to pray—
To tell You the truth, God,
  I don't know what to say . . .
I just know I am lonely
  And vaguely disturbed,
Bewildered and restless,
  Confused and perturbed . . .
And they tell me that prayer
  Helps to quiet the mind
And to unburden the heart
  For in stillness we find
A newborn assurance
  That Someone does care
And Someone does answer
  Each small sincere prayer!

. . . The prayer of a righteous man has great power in its effects.
James 5:16

In Hours of Discouragement
God Is Our Encouragement

The Lord is our salvation,
And our strength in every fight,
Our redeemer and protector,
Our eternal guiding light.
He has promised to sustain us,
He's our refuge from all harms,
And underneath this refuge
Are the everlasting arms,
So cast your burden on Him,
Seek His counsel when distressed,
And go to Him for comfort
When you're lonely and oppressed,
For God is our encouragement
In trouble and in trials,
And in suffering and in sorrow
He will turn our tears to smiles.

The eternal God is your dwelling place, and underneath are the everlasting arms. . . .

Deuteronomy 33:27

This, Too, Will Pass Away

If I can endure for this minute
Whatever is happening to me,
No matter how heavy my heart is
Or how dark the moment may be,
If I can remain calm and quiet
With all my world crashing about me,
If I can but keep on believing
What I know in my heart to be true—
That darkness will fade with the morning
And that this will pass away, too—
Then nothing in life can defeat me
For as long as this knowledge remains
I can suffer whatever is happening
For I know God will break all the chains
That are binding me tight in the darkness
And trying to fill me with fear,
For there is no night without dawning
And I know that my morning is near.

Again Jesus spoke to them, saying, "I am the light of the world; he who follows me will not walk in darkness, but will have the light of life."
                                                              John 8:12

"Lead Us
From Night to
Never-Ending
Day"

God of Our Fathers

God of our fathers, whose almighty hand
Leads forth in beauty all the starry band
Of shining worlds in splendor thru the skies,
Our grateful songs before Thy throne arise.

Thy love divine hath led us in the past,
In this free land by Thee our lot is cast;
Be Thou our ruler, guardian, guide, and stay,
Thy word our law, Thy paths our chosen way.

From war's alarms, from deadly pestilence,
Be Thy strong arm our ever-sure defense;
Thy true religion in our hearts increase,
Thy bounteous goodness nourish us in peace.

Refresh Thy people on their toilsome way,
Lead us from night to never-ending day;
Fill all our lives with love and grace divine,
And glory, laud, and praise be ever Thine!

DANIEL C. ROBERTS

In 1876, one hundred years after the signing of the Declaration of Independence, Daniel C. Roberts, pastor of a small rural church in Brandon, Vermont, decided to write a hymn to help the little New England community celebrate the event.

A humble man, he had served in the Civil War before entering the ministry. Throughout his life, he served various small churches in New England. Once he wrote, "I remain a country Parson, known only within my own small world."

The hymn that he wrote for Brandon, Vermont, was sung at the Fourth of July celebration in that town, and then it was forgotten.

But more than a decade later, when he heard that his denomination was revising its hymnal and was looking for new American hymns to insert, Daniel Roberts submitted his hymn anonymously. He didn't think it had much of a chance of being included in the Episcopalian hymnal.

However, not only was "God of Our Fathers" accepted into the hymnal but it was also chosen as the official hymn commemorating the centennial of the adoption of the Constitution.

The Soul of Man

Every man has a deep heart need
That should be filled with doctrine and creed,
For the soul of man knows nothing more
Than just that he is longing for
A haven that is safe and sure,
A fortress where he feels secure,
An island in this sea of strife
Away from all the storms of life.
O God of love, who sees us all,
You are so great! We are so small!
Hear man's universal prayer
Crying to You in despair—
"Save my soul and grant me peace,
Let my restless murmurings cease,
God of love—Forgive! Forgive!
Teach me how to truly live,
Ask me not my race or creed,
Just take me in my hour of need,
And let me know You love me, too,
And that I am a part of You" . . .
And someday may man realize
That all the earth, the seas, and skies
Belong to God who made us all,
The rich, the poor, the great, the small,
And in the Father's holy sight
No man is yellow, black, or white,
And peace on earth cannot be found
Until we meet on common ground.

What More Can You Ask?

God's love endureth forever—
What a wonderful thing to know
When the tides of life run against you
And your spirit is downcast and low.
God's kindness is ever around you,
Always ready to freely impart
Strength to your faltering spirit,
Cheer to your lonely heart.
God's presence is ever beside you,
As near as the reach of your hand,
You have but to tell Him your troubles,
There is nothing He won't understand.
And knowing God's love is unfailing,
And His mercy unending and great,
You have but to trust in His promise—
God comes not too soon or too late.
So wait with a heart that is patient
For the goodness of God to prevail,
For never do prayers go unanswered,
And His mercy and love never fail.

For I am sure that neither death, nor life, nor angels, nor principalities, nor things present, nor things to come, nor powers, nor height, nor depth, nor anything else in all creation, will be able to separate us from the love of God in Christ Jesus our Lord.

Romans 8:38, 39

Never Despair
God's Always There!

In sickness or health,
In suffering or pain,
In storm-laden skies,
In sunshine and rain
God always is there
To lighten your way
And lead you through darkness
To a much brighter day.

But know that the Lord has set apart the godly for himself; the Lord hears when I call to him.

Psalm 4:3

God's Love

God's love is like an island
In life's ocean vast and wide,
A peaceful, quiet shelter
From the restless, rising tide.

God's love is like an anchor
When the angry billows roll,
A mooring in the storms of life,
A stronghold for the soul.

God's love is like a fortress
And we seek protection there
When the waves of tribulation
Seem to drown us in despair.

God's love is like a harbor
Where our souls can find sweet rest
From the struggle and the tension
Of life's fast and futile quest.

God's love is like a beacon
Burning bright with faith and prayer
And through the changing scenes of life
We can find a haven there!

"The Lord is my rock, and my fortress, and my deliverer."
2 Samuel 22:2

It's Me Again, God

Remember me, God?
I come every day
Just to talk with You, Lord,
And to learn how to pray.
You make me feel welcome,
You reach out Your hand,
I need never explain
For You understand.
I come to You frightened
And burdened with care
So lonely and lost
And so filled with despair,
And suddenly, Lord,
I'm no longer afraid,
My burden is lighter
And the dark shadows fade.
O God, what a comfort
To know that You care
And to know when I seek You
You will always be there!

Cast your burden on the Lord, and he will sustain you; he will never permit the righteous to be moved.

Psalm 55:22

Trouble

God, help us to accept Your love
    that You offer us so freely
And make us ever thankful
    that You give it lavishly.
But make us also conscious
    that Your love comes in many ways
And not always just as happiness
    and bright and shining days.
For often You send trouble
    and we foolishly reject it,
Not realizing that it is Your will
    and we should joyously accept it.
And in trouble and in gladness
    we can always hear Your voice
If we listen in the silence
    and find a reason to rejoice.

In the day of my trouble I seek the Lord; in the night my hand is stretched out without wearying; my soul refuses to be comforted.

Psalm 77:2

94

In Him We Live and Move and Have Our Being

We walk in a world that is strange and unknown
And in the midst of the crowd we still feel alone,
We question our purpose, our part, and our place
In this vast land of mystery suspended in space,
We probe and explore and try hard to explain
The tumult of thoughts that our minds entertain,
But all of our probings and complex explanations
Of man's inner feelings and fears and frustrations
Still leave us engulfed in the mystery of life
With all of its struggles and suffering and strife,
Unable to fathom what tomorrow will bring,
But there is one truth to which we can cling,
For while life's a mystery man can't understand
The Great Giver of Life is holding our hand
And safe in His care there is no need for seeing
For in Him we live and move and have our being.

"In him we live and move and have our being"; as even some of your poets have said, "For we are indeed his offspring."

Acts 17:28

95

On the Wings of Prayer

Just close your eyes and open your heart
And feel your worries and cares depart,
Just yield yourself to the Father above
And let Him hold you secure in His love.
For life on earth grows more involved
With endless problems that can't be solved,
But God only asks us to do our best,
Then He will take over and finish the rest.
So when you are tired, discouraged, and blue,
There's always one door that is open to you,
And that is the door to the house of prayer
And you'll find God waiting to meet you there,
And the house of prayer is no farther away
Than the quiet spot where you kneel and pray.
For the heart is a temple when God is there
As we place ourselves in His loving care,
And He hears every prayer and answers each one
When we pray in His name, "Thy will be done."
And the burdens that seemed too heavy to bear
Are lifted away on the wings of prayer.

. . . *"For my house shall be called a house of prayer for all peoples."*
Isaiah 56:7

96

Somebody Cares

Somebody cares and always will,
The world forgets but God loves you still,
You cannot go beyond His love
No matter what you're guilty of.
For God forgives until the end,
He is your faithful, loyal Friend,
And though you try to hide your face
There is no shelter anyplace
That can escape His watchful eye,
For on the earth and in the sky
He's ever present and always there
To take you in His tender care
And bind the wounds and mend the breaks
When all the world around forsakes.
Somebody cares and loves you still
And God is the Someone who always will.

''For the mountains may depart and the hills be removed, but my steadfast love shall not depart from you, and my covenant of peace shall not be removed, says the Lord, who has compassion on you.''

Isaiah 54:10

"I Love Thy Rocks and Rills, Thy Woods and Templed Hills"

My Country, 'Tis of Thee

My country, 'tis of thee,
Sweet land of liberty,
Of thee I sing:
Land where my fathers died,
Land of the pilgrims' pride,
From ev'ry mountainside
Let freedom ring!

My native country, thee,
Land of the noble free,
Thy name I love.
I love thy rocks and rills,
Thy woods and templed hills;
My heart with rapture thrills
Like that above.

Let music swell the breeze,
And ring from all the trees
Sweet freedom's song.
Let mortal tongues awake;
Let all that breathe partake;
Let rocks their silence break,
The sound prolong.

Our fathers' God, to Thee,
Author of liberty,
To Thee we sing:
Long may our land be bright
With freedom's holy light;
Protect us by Thy might,
Great God, our King!

SAMUEL FRANCIS SMITH

Samuel Francis Smith was a twenty-three-year-old seminary student when he wrote the patriotic hymn that begins "My Country, 'Tis of Thee."

Later, Smith became a Baptist pastor, the editor of a missionary magazine, and a gifted linguist who was accomplished in fifteen languages. At the age of eighty-six, he began studying Russian.

Because Smith had this linguistic gift as a seminary student, Lowell Mason, the music educator, came to him for help. Mason had been studying how teachers in Europe and in England trained boys and girls in music. Just back from Europe, he had brought with him many German songs which had to be translated into English.

Young Samuel Smith was honored to be asked by the noted musicologist, and he began his assignment eagerly. As he translated, there was one German song that caught his attention. There was both simplicity and majesty to it. It went like this:

> God bless our native land.
> Firm may she ever stand
> In storm and night.

The unusual cadence of the song captured his attention and he decided to write a patriotic hymn for America based on the same meter. Quickly the words came to him. So it was that in February 1832, Smith wrote the lyrics in a half hour on a piece of scrap paper.

The next time he went to Boston to see Lowell Mason, he gave him the lyrics and then forgot about them.

But on the Fourth of July, Smith was in Boston again. He writes, "As I was passing Park Street Church, I was attracted by the sound of music. I entered and found the building filled with boys and girls engaged in celebrating the day." He noticed that his friend Lowell Mason was directing the children's choir, but what he noticed next surprised him even more. "Glancing over the program held by the person in front of me, I saw that the last piece was a song entitled, 'My Country, 'Tis of Thee.'"

The Heavens Declare the Glory of God

You ask me how I know it's true
  That there is a living God—
A God who rules the universe,
  The sky . . . the sea . . . the sod;
A God who holds all creatures
  In the hollow of His hand;
A God who put infinity
  In one tiny grain of sand;
A God who made the seasons—
  Winter, summer, fall, and spring,
And put His flawless rhythm
  Into each created thing;
A God who hangs the sun out
  Slowly with the break of day,
And gently takes the stars in
  And puts the night away;
A God whose mighty handiwork
  Defies the skill of man,
For no architect can alter
  God's perfect master plan—
What better answers are there
  To prove His Holy Being
Than the wonders all around us
  That are ours just for the seeing.

My God Is No Stranger

God is no stranger in a faraway place,
He's as close as the wind that blows 'cross my face,
It's true I can't see the wind as it blows
But I feel it around me and my heart surely knows
That God's mighty hand can be felt every minute
For there is nothing on earth that God isn't in it—
The sky and the stars, the waves and the sea,
The dew on the grass, the leaves on a tree
Are constant reminders of God and His nearness,
Proclaiming His presence with crystal-like clearness—
So how could I think God was far, far away
When I feel Him beside me every hour of the day,
And I've plenty of reasons to know God's my Friend
And this is one friendship that time cannot end!

And he said, "My presence will go with you, and I will give you rest."
Exodus 33:14

104

The Masterpiece

Framed by the vast unlimited sky
Bordered by mighty waters,
Sheltered by beautiful woodland groves,
Scented with flowers that bloom, and die
Protected by giant mountain peaks
The lands of the great unknown—
Snowcapped and towering—a nameless place
That beckons man on as the gold he seeks.
Bubbling with life and earthly joys
Reeking with pain and mortal strife.
Dotted with wealth and material gains
Built on ideals of girls and boys.
Streaked with toil, opportunity's banner unfurled
Stands out the masterpiece of art—
Painted by the one great God
A picture of the world!

Sing to him, sing praises to him, tell of all his wonderful works!
                                                      Psalm 105:2

A Soldier Meets God in the Morning

The earth is the Lord's
and the fulness thereof.
It speaks of His greatness,
it sings of His love,
And each day at dawning
I lift my heart high
And raise up my eyes
to the infinite sky . . .
I watch the night vanish
as a new day is born,
And I hear the birds sing
on the wings of the morn,
I see the dew glisten
in crystal-like splendor
While God, with a touch
that is gentle and tender,
Wraps up the night
and softly tucks it away
And hangs out the sun
to herald a new day . . .
And so I give thanks
and my heart kneels to pray—
"God keep me and guide me
and go with me today."

Fear not, for I am with you, be not dismayed, for I am your God; I will strengthen you, I will help you, I will uphold you with my victorious right hand.

Isaiah 41:10

God Whispering

Each time you look up in the sky
Or watch the fluffy clouds drift by,
Or feel the sunshine warm and bright,
Or watch the dark night turn to light,
Or hear a bluebird happily sing,
Or see the winter turn to spring,
Or stop to pick a daffodil,
Or gather violets on some hill . . .
Or touch a leaf or see a tree,
It's all God whispering, "This is Me . . .
And I am faith and I am light
And in Me there shall be no night."

*But I trust in thee, O Lord, I say, "Thou art my God." My times are in thy
hand; deliver me from the hand of my enemies and persecutors!*

Psalm 31:14, 15

A Thankful Heart

Take nothing for granted, for whenever you do
The joy of enjoying is lessened for you,
For we rob our own lives much more than we know
When we fail to respond or in any way show
Our thanks for the blessings that daily are ours,
The warmth of the sun, the fragrance of flowers,
The beauty of twilight, the freshness of dawn,
The coolness of dew on a green velvet lawn,
The kind little deeds so thoughtfully done,
The favors of friends and the love that someone
Unselfishly gives us in a myriad of ways,
Expecting no payment and no words of praise—
Oh, great is our loss when we no longer find
A thankful response to things of this kind,
For the joy of enjoying
    and the fullness of living
Are found in the heart
    that is filled with thanksgiving.

For everything created by God is good, and nothing is to be rejected if it is received with thanksgiving; for then it is consecrated by the word of God and prayer.

1 Timothy 4:4, 5

A Prayer of Thanks

Thank You, God, for everything
    I've experienced here on earth—
Thank You for protecting me
    from the moment of my birth—
And thank You for the beauty
    around me everywhere,
The gentle rain and glistening dew,
    the sunshine and the air,
The joyous gift of "feeling"
    the soul's soft, whispering voice
That speaks to me from deep within
    and makes my heart rejoice—
O God, no words are great enough
    to thank You for just living,
And that is why every day
    is a day for real thanksgiving.

The earth is the Lord's and the fulness thereof, the world and those who dwell therein; for he has founded it upon the seas, and established it upon the rivers.

Psalm 24:1, 2

Our Lavish God

God is so lavish
In all that He's done
To make this great world
Such a wonderful one . . .

His mountains are high
His oceans are deep
And vast and unmeasured
The prairie lands sweep . . .

His heavens are dotted
With uncounted jewels
For joy without measure
Is one of God's rules.

Thou hast multiplied, O Lord my God, thy wondrous deeds and thy thoughts toward us; none can compare with thee!

Psalms 40:5

After the Winter God Sends the Spring

Springtime is a season
Of hope and joy and cheer,
There's beauty all around us
To see and touch and hear.
So, no matter how downhearted
And discouraged we may be,
New hope is born when we behold
Leaves budding on a tree,
Or when we see a timid flower
Push through the frozen sod
And open wide in glad surprise
Its petaled eyes to God.
For this is just God saying,
"Lift up your eyes to Me,
And the bleakness of your spirit,
Like the budding springtime tree,
Will lose its wintry darkness
And your heavy heart will sing."
For God never sends the winter
Without the joy of spring.

"For lo, the winter is past, the rain is over and gone. The flowers appear on the earth, the time of singing has come, and the voice of the turtledove is heard in our land."

Song of Solomon 2:11, 12

Let us love forever
This land of liberty.
Let us accept our duty
To keep our country free.

May our faith in God never waiver
And our loyalty remain strong and true.
May the principles that we favor
Remain with us all life through.

VJR